Bala Kids
An imprint of Shambhala Publications, Inc.
4720 Walnut Street
Boulder, Colorado 80301
www.shambhala.com

9 8 7 6 5 4 3 2 1

First Edition
Printed in China

⊗ This edition is printed on acid-free paper that meets the
American National Standards Institute Z39.48 Standard.
♻ Shambhala Publications makes every effort to print on recycled paper.
For more information please visit www.shambhala.com.
Bala Kids is distributed worldwide by Penguin Random House, Inc., and its subsidiaries.

Library of Congress Cataloging-in-Publication Data
Names: Ricard, Matthieu, author. | Hall, Becca, illustrator.
Title: Our animal neighbors: compassion for every furry, slimy, prickly
creature on earth / Matthieu Ricard, Jason Gruhl;
illustrated by Becca Hall.
Description: First edition. | Boulder, Colorado: Bala Kids, 2020. |
Audience: Age 4–8. | Audience: K to Grade 3.
Identifiers: LCCN 2018060007 | ISBN 9781611807233 (hardcover: alk. paper)
Subjects: LCSH: Animals (Philosophy)—Juvenile literature. | Human-animal
relationships—Philosophy—Juvenile literature. | Compassion—Religious
aspects—Juvenile literature.
Classification: LCC B105.A55 R53 2020 | DDC 179/.3—dc23
LC record available at https://lccn.loc.gov/2018060007

OUR ANIMAL NEIGHBORS

COMPASSION FOR EVERY FURRY, SLIMY, PRICKLY CREATURE ON EARTH

WRITTEN BY MATTHIEU RICARD
AND JASON GRUHL

ILLUSTRATED BY BECCA HALL

bala kids

Neighbors come in all shapes, colors, and kinds.
Some are friendly. Some are grouchy.
Some *never* stop talking. And some love to be left alone.

Yet no matter who we are,
we're all part of the same
neighborhood.

And while animal neighbors and human neighbors can *seem* quite different—

we have different **skills** that help us **survive,**

INTELLIGENCE

SENSE OF DIRECTION

USING TOOLS

NIGHT VISION

SONAR

COUNTING

STRENGTH

SHAPE-SHIFTING

we have **wildly** different likes and needs,

and we feel at home in
very different places—

in this big,
beautiful
neighborhood
called Earth,

we all

belong.

In fact, you have more in common with your neighbors than you think! We all need . . .

FOOD AND WATER

HEALTH AND REST

CLEAN AIR AND SHELTER

We all enjoy . . .

FAMILY AND FRIENDSHIP,

 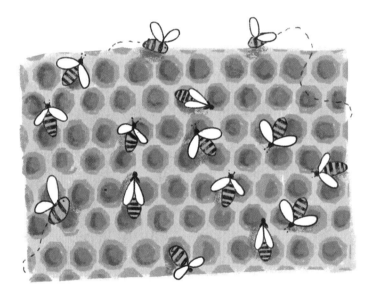

HOME AND WORK,

COMMUNICATION AND PLAY.

And whether we have hands or hooves,
skin or scales . . . no one wants to be . . .

And *everyone* wants to be . . .

FREE,

SAFE,

AND FEEL JOYFUL,

AND VALUED;

HAPPY, AND . . .

Good neighbors always
look out for one another.

And when we look with our eyes *and* our hearts,
we can act with love and compassion toward all beings . . .

even the **grouchy** ones.

So look around and wave to your neighbors—

THE FURRY,   THE PRICKLY,   THE SLIMY,   THE SHY,

—next door, across town,
in the sea,
in the sky . . .

and across this BIG, beautiful
neighborhood called Earth.

This is our home, and we are
all neighbors.

FACTS, FIGURES & THINGS TO PONDER

WE'RE ACTUALLY ALL RELATED! OVER 3 BILLION YEARS AGO, YOUR GREAT-GREAT-GREAT-GREAT-GREAT GRANDMOTHER WAS A SINGLE CELL! WE'VE COME A LONG WAY TOGETHER AND EVOLVED IN DIFFERENT WAYS, BUT IT'S ALL US!

THE BILLION TONS OF GRAIN FED TO ANIMALS THAT BECOME MEAT COULD FEED 1.5 BILLION UNDERNOURISHED PEOPLE EACH YEAR.

EATING A PLANT-BASED DIET SAVES HUMAN LIVES, TOO! EATING ANIMALS AND ANIMAL PRODUCTS INCREASES ONE'S RISK OF CANCER, HEART DISEASE, DIABETES, AND OBESITY.

IF ALL THE PEOPLE OF NORTH AMERICA STOPPED EATING MEAT ONE DAY A WEEK, IT WOULD BE POSSIBLE TO FEED 25 MILLION HUNGRY PEOPLE EVERY DAY FOR AN ENTIRE YEAR!

WHILE PLANES, TRAINS, AND AUTOMOBILES CREATE TONS OF POLLUTION, THE MEAT INDUSTRY CONTRIBUTES MORE TO CLIMATE CHANGE THAN ALL THE FORMS OF TRANSPORTATION COMBINED.

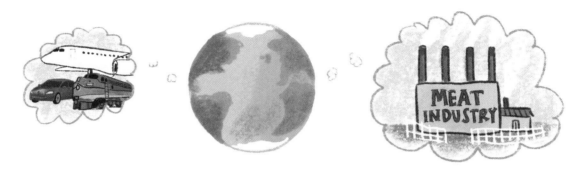

SO MANY PEOPLE AROUND THE WORLD LOVE THEIR CATS, DOGS, BIRDS, AND RABBITS AS PETS, BUT THEY DON'T EXTEND THIS SAME CARE TO THE REST OF THE ANIMAL KINGDOM. IT JUST DOESN'T MAKE SENSE: WHY DO WE HELP AND LOVE SOME KINDS OF ANIMALS WHILE CAUSING OR EXCUSING THE DEATHS OF OTHERS?

IN THE HISTORY OF THE HUMAN RACE, 100 BILLION PEOPLE HAVE LIVED ON EARTH. HUMANS KILL THAT SAME NUMBER OF ANIMALS EVERY TWO MONTHS TO EAT, WEAR, OR EXPERIMENT ON.

100 BILLION
(TOTAL IN HISTORY!)

100 BILLION
(KILLED IN TWO MONTHS)

THERE ARE 550 MILLION TO 600 MILLION VEGETARIANS IN THE WORLD... AND COUNTING.

I SHOULD COMBAT THE PAIN
OF OTHERS BECAUSE IT IS PAIN LIKE
MY OWN. I SHOULD WORK FOR THE
GOOD OF OTHERS BECAUSE THEY ARE
LIKE ME, LIVING BEINGS.

– SHANTIDEVA

RESOURCES

For more information on helping our animal neighbors,
please visit the following websites:

- humanesociety.org
- janegoodall.org
- karuna-shechen.org

- kids.nationalgeographic.com
- onegreenplanet.org
- petakids.com